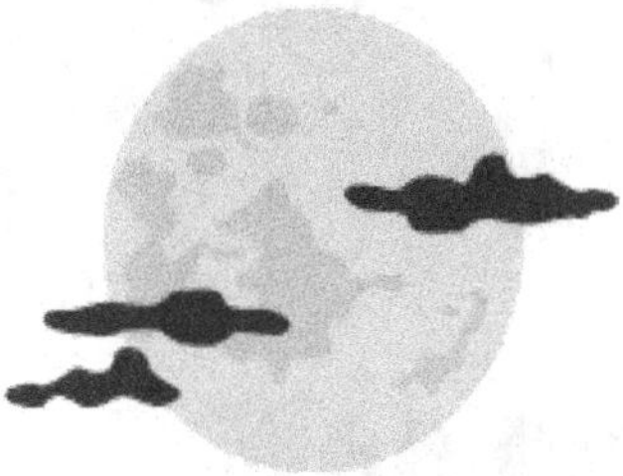

THIS BOOK BELONGS TO:

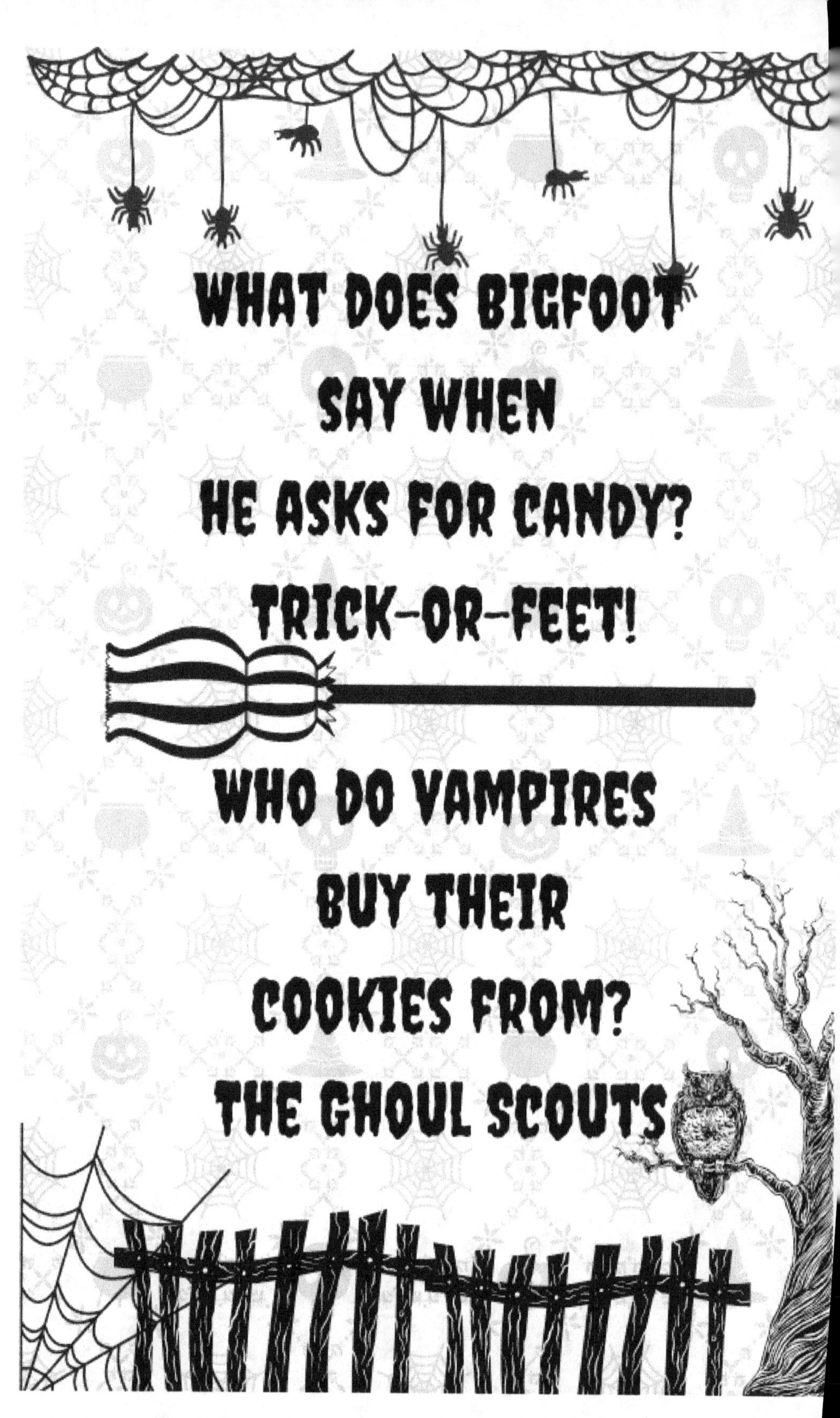
WHAT DOES BIGFOOT
SAY WHEN
HE ASKS FOR CANDY?
TRICK-OR-FEET!

WHO DO VAMPIRES
BUY THEIR
COOKIES FROM?
THE GHOUL SCOUTS

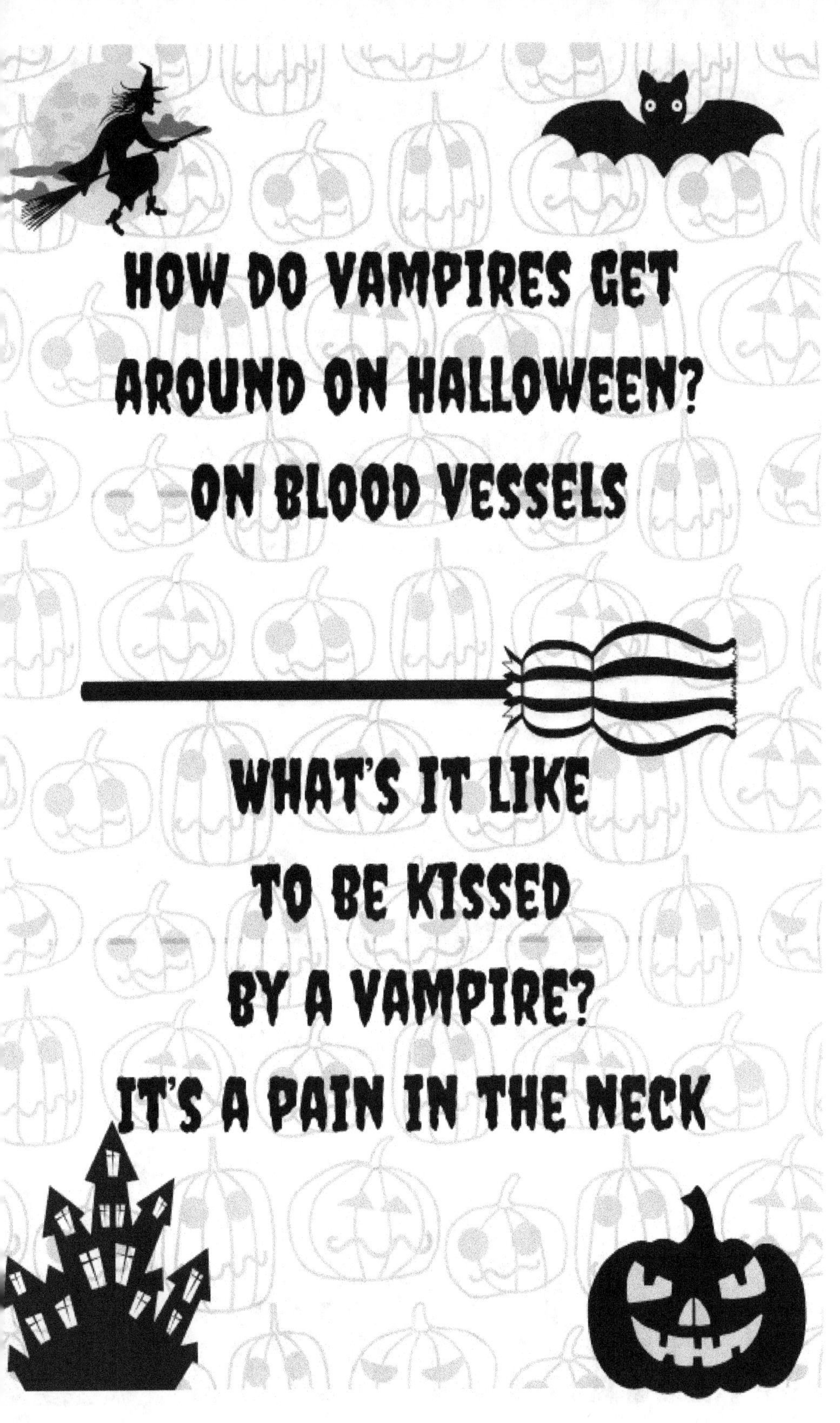

HOW DO VAMPIRES GET
AROUND ON HALLOWEEN?
ON BLOOD VESSELS

WHAT'S IT LIKE
TO BE KISSED
BY A VAMPIRE?
IT'S A PAIN IN THE NECK

WHAT IS A GHOST'S FAVORITE PIE?

BOOBERRY PIE!

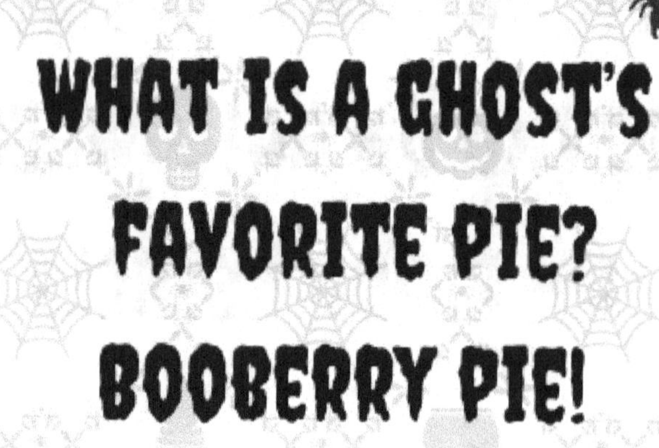

WHAT DO VAMPIRES TAKE WHEN THEY ARE SICK?

COFFIN DROPS!

WHAT'S IT CALLED WHEN A VAMPIRE HAS TROUBLE WITH HIS HOUSE? A GRAVE PROBLEM
WHAT DO YOU GET WHEN YOU CROSS A VAMPIRE AND A SNOWMAN? FROSTBITE

WHAT DO YOU CALL A WITCH'S GARAGE?
A BROOM CLOSET

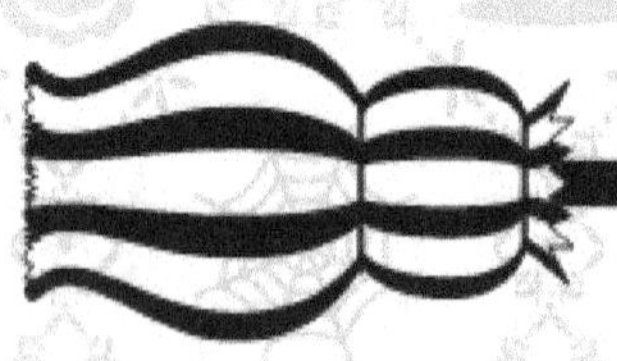

WHAT DO GHOSTS EAT FOR SUPPER?
SPOOKETI

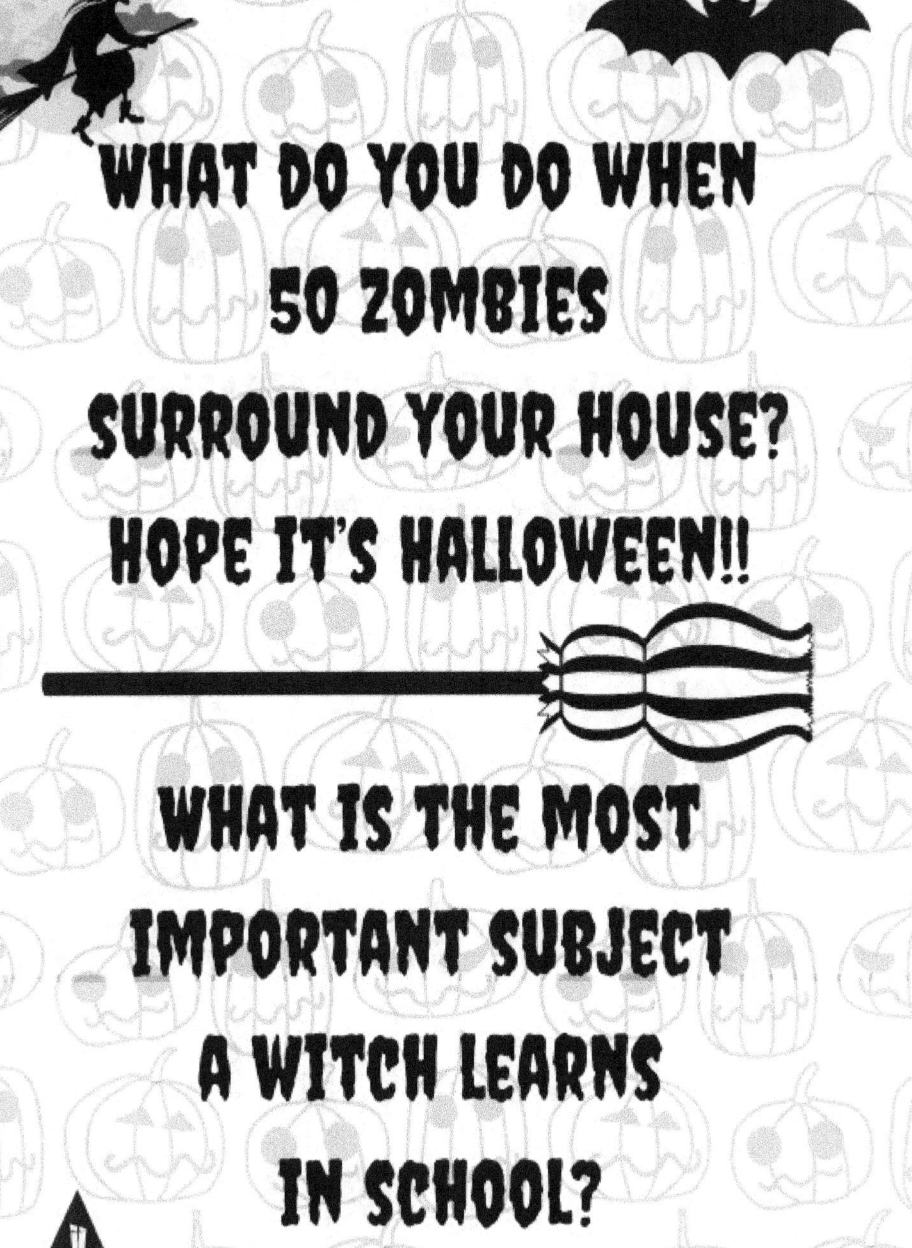
WHAT DO YOU DO WHEN
50 ZOMBIES
SURROUND YOUR HOUSE?
HOPE IT'S HALLOWEEN!!

WHAT IS THE MOST
IMPORTANT SUBJECT
A WITCH LEARNS
IN SCHOOL?
SPELLING

WHAT'S A WITCH'S FAVORITE MAKEUP?
MA-SCARE-A

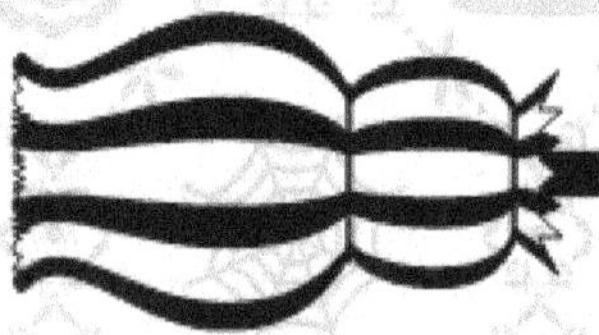

WHAT DID THE GHOST SAY TO THE OTHER GHOST?
DO YOU BELIEVE IN HUMANS

WHAT GOES AROUND
A HAUNTED HOUSE
AND NEVER STOPS?
A FENCE

WHY DO GHOSTS
MAKE GOOD
CHEERLEADERS?
BECAUSE THEY HAVE
A LOT OF SPIRIT

WHAT KIND OF PANTS DO GHOSTS WEAR?
BOO-JEANS

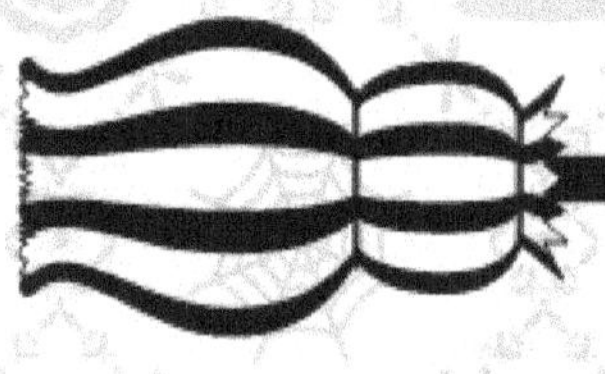

WHAT DOES A WITCH USE TO KEEP HER HAIR UP?
SCARESPRAY!

WHAT DOES A SKELETON
SAY BEFORE DINNER?
BONE APPETIT!

WHEN IS IT BAD LUCK
TO BE FOLLOWED
BY A BLACK CAT?
WHEN YOU'RE A MOUSE

WHAT DO BIRDS SAY ON HALLOWEEN?
TRICK OR TWEET!

WHO DOES DRACULA GET LETTERS FROM?
HIS FANG CLUB

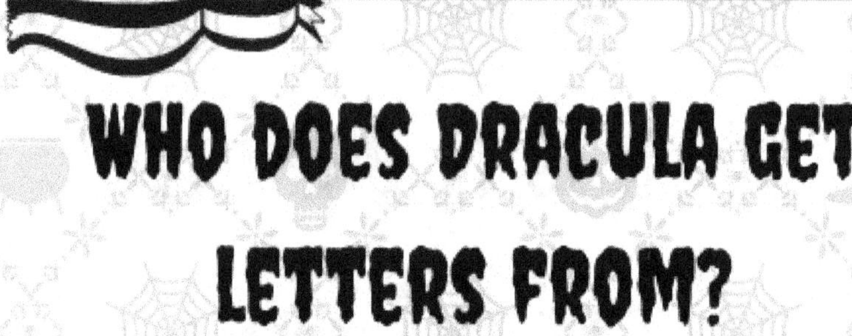

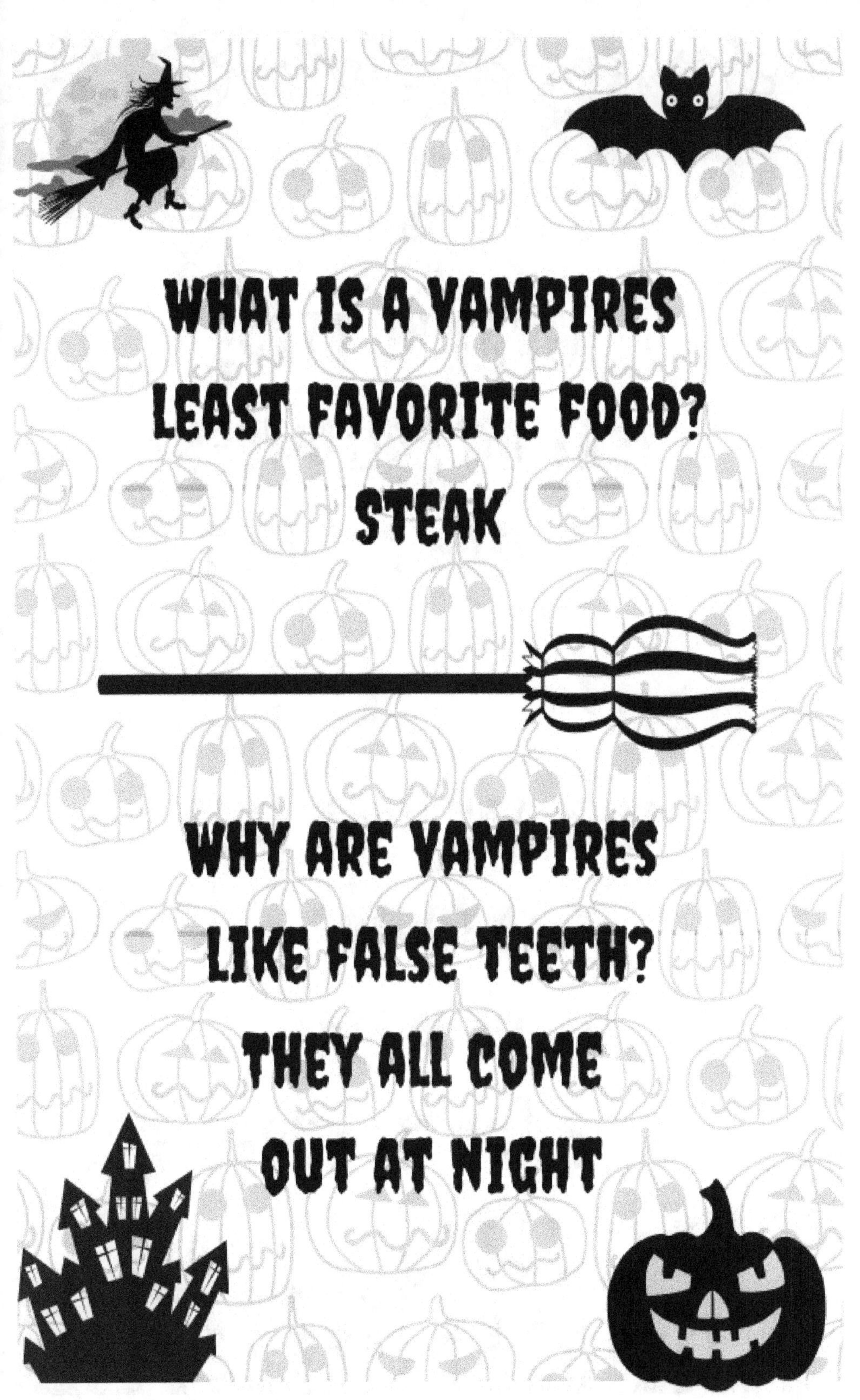
WHAT IS A VAMPIRES
LEAST FAVORITE FOOD?
STEAK

WHY ARE VAMPIRES
LIKE FALSE TEETH?
THEY ALL COME
OUT AT NIGHT

WHAT DO BIRDS SAY ON HALLOWEEN?
TWICK O TWEET

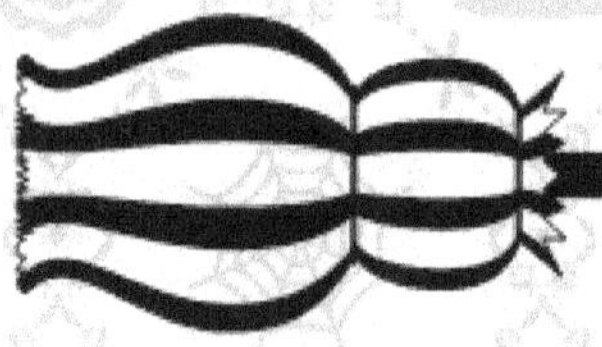

WHY ARE VAMPIRES STUPID?
BECAUSE THEY ARE ALL SUCKERS

WHERE DOES A GHOST
GO ON SATURDAY NIGHT?
ANYWHERE WHERE
HE CAN
BOO-GIE

WHAT DO YOU GET
WHEN YOU DROP
A PUMPKIN?!
SQUASH!

WHAT IS A VAMPIRE'S FAVORITE FRUIT?
A NECKTARINE

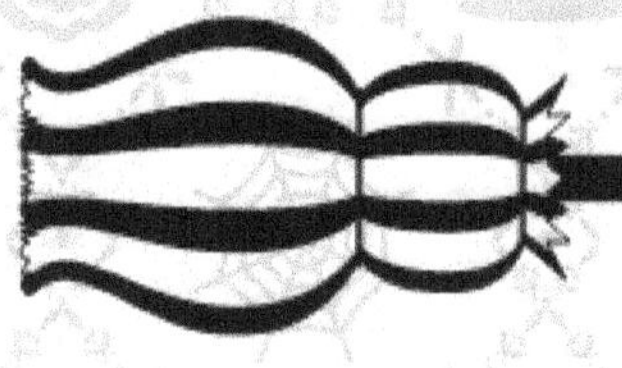

WHERE DO VAMPIRES KEEP THEIR MONEY?
THE BLOOD BANK!!!

WHAT IS A VAMPIRE'S FAVOURITE ICE CREAM FLAVOR?!
VEINILLA

WHO DID FRANKENSTEIN TAKE TO THE PROM?
HIS GHOUL FRIEND

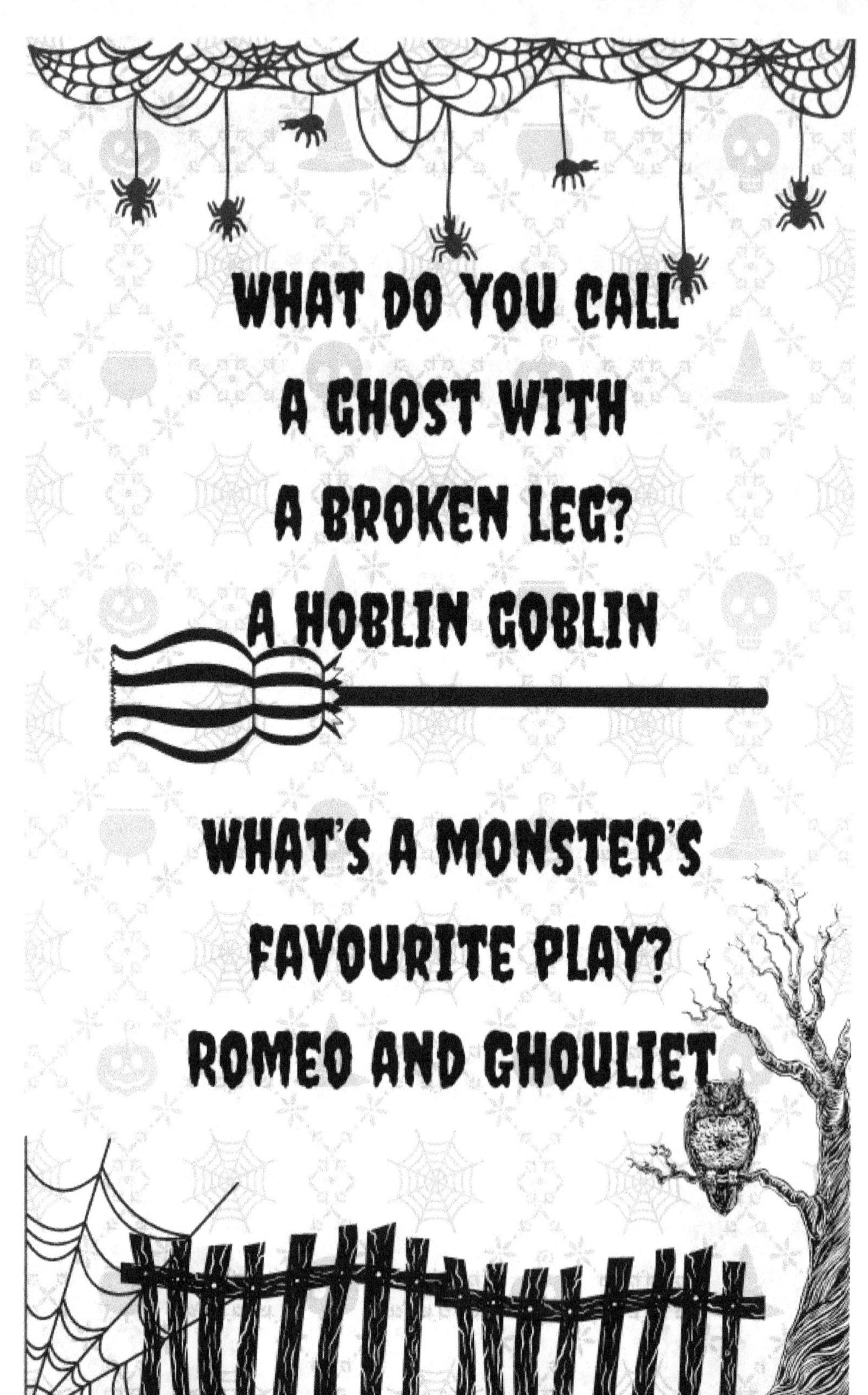

WHAT DO YOU CALL
A GHOST WITH
A BROKEN LEG?
A HOBLIN GOBLIN

WHAT'S A MONSTER'S
FAVOURITE PLAY?
ROMEO AND GHOULIET

WHY WAS THE MUMMY SO TENSE?
HE WAS ALL WOUND UP

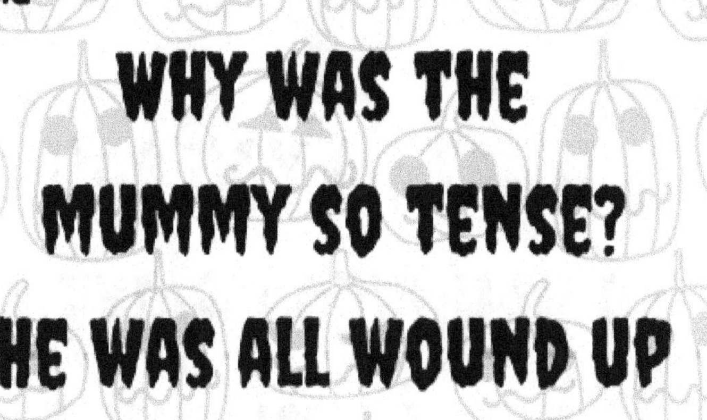

WHAT DID THE SKELETON SAY TO THE BARTENDER?
I'LL HAVE TWO BEERS AND A MOP

WHAT DO YOU CALL
A HAUNTED CHICKEN?
A POULTRY-GEIST

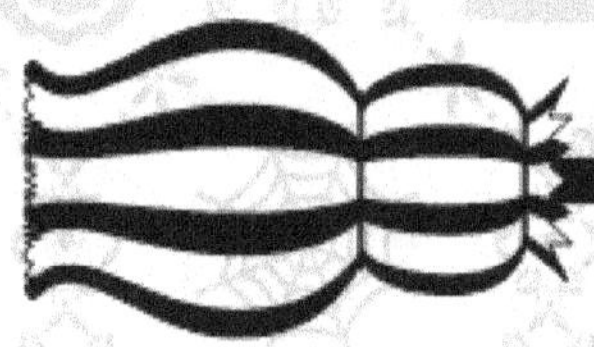

WHERE DO MUMMIES
GO FOR A SWIM?
TO THE DEAD SEA

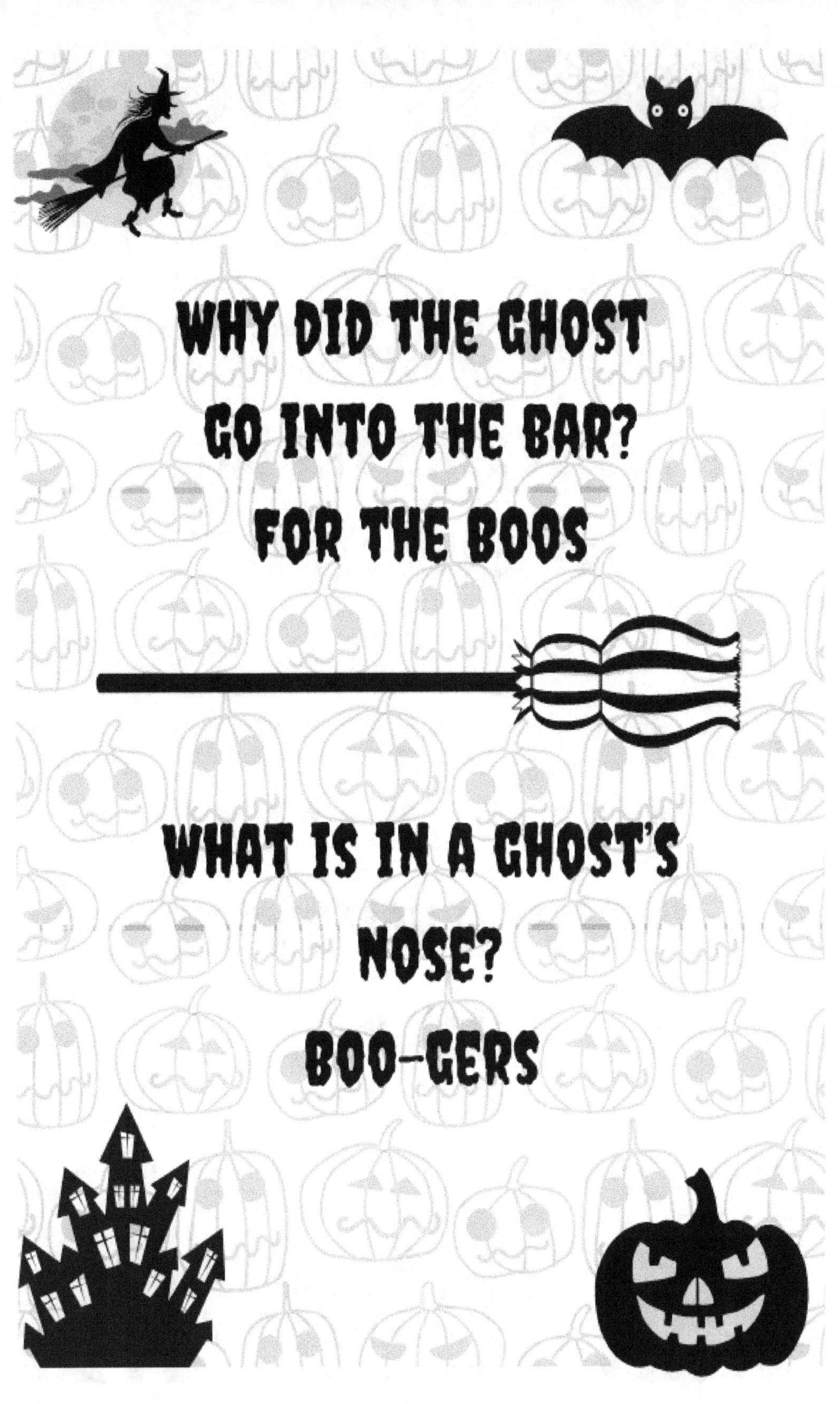

WHY DID THE GHOST
GO INTO THE BAR?
FOR THE BOOS

WHAT IS IN A GHOST'S
NOSE?
BOO-GERS

WHERE DO BABY GHOSTS GO DURING THE DAY?
DAYSCARE CENTRES

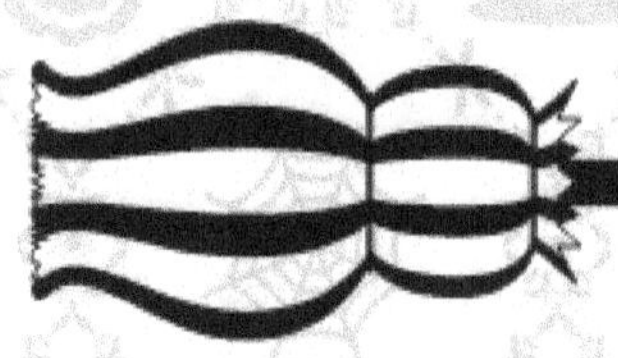

WHAT DO BABY GHOSTS WEAR ON HALLOWEEN?
PILLOWCASES

WHAT DOES A PANDA GHOST EAT?
BAM-BOO!
WHAT'S A GHOST'S FAVORITE DESSERT?
I-SCREAM!

WHERE DO GHOSTS BUY THEIR HALLOWEEN CANDY?

AT THE GHOST-ERY STORE

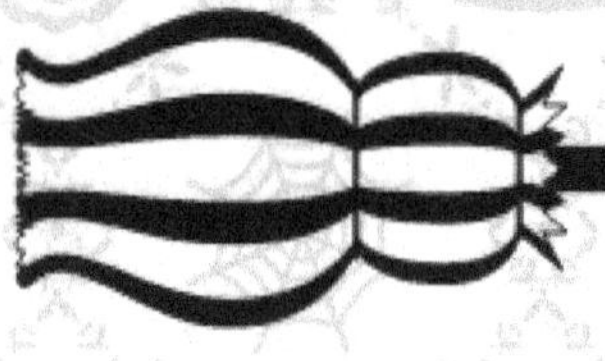

WHAT DO OWLS SAY WHEN THEY GO TRICK OR TREATING?

HAPPY OWL-WEEN!

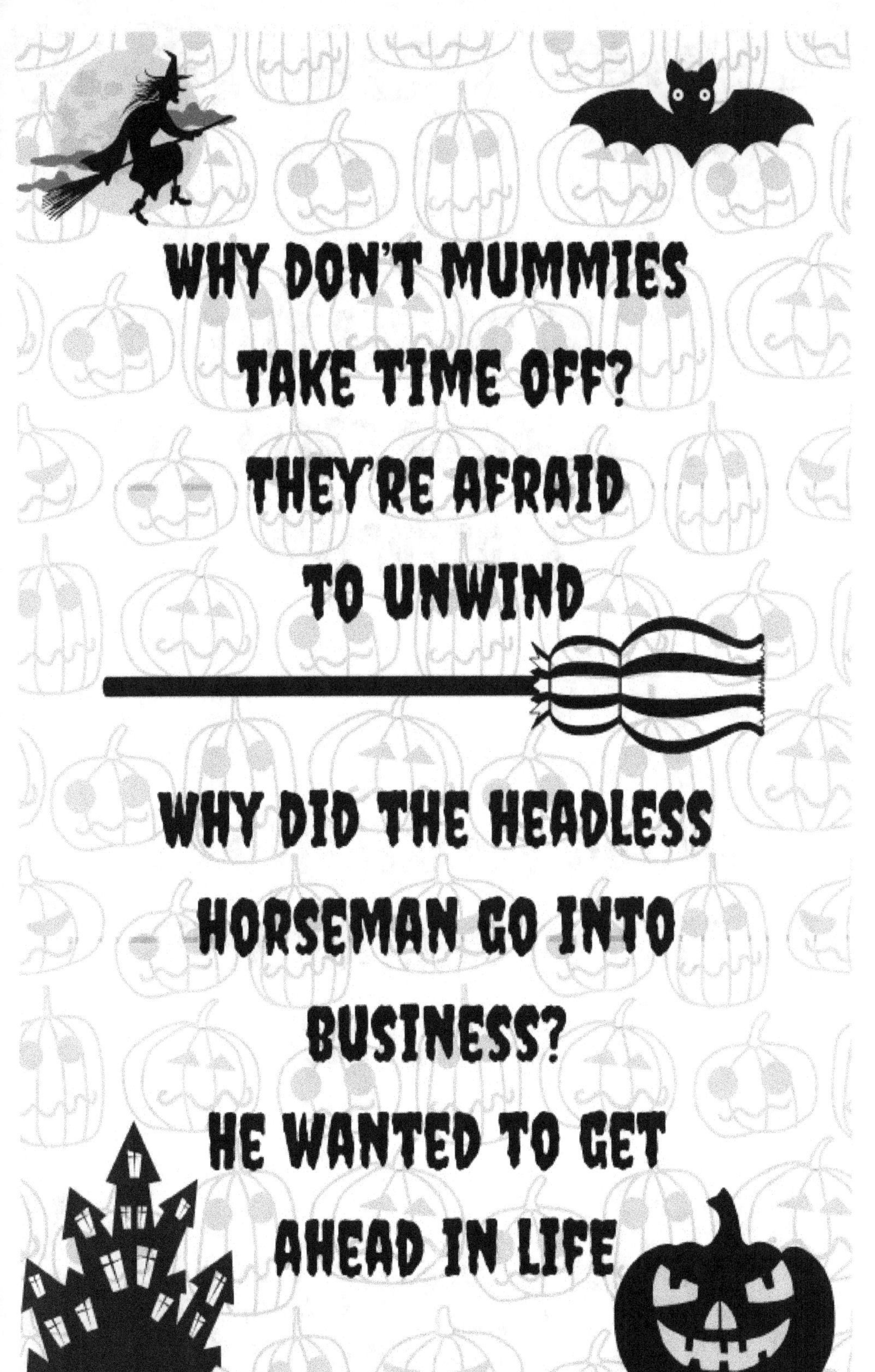

WHY DON'T MUMMIES TAKE TIME OFF?
THEY'RE AFRAID TO UNWIND

WHY DID THE HEADLESS HORSEMAN GO INTO BUSINESS?
HE WANTED TO GET AHEAD IN LIFE

WHAT DO GHOSTS GIVE OUT TO TRICK OR TREATERS?
BOOBERRIES!

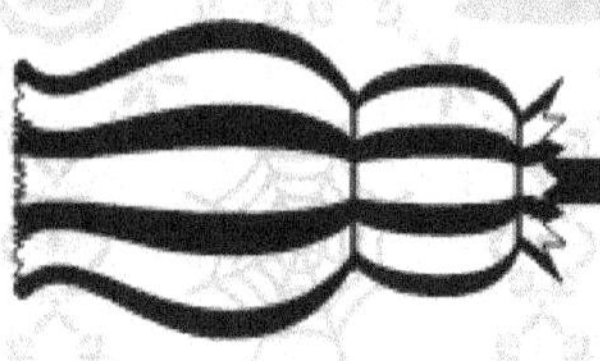

WHO DID FRANKENSTEIN GO TRICK OR TREATING WITH?
HIS GHOUL FRIEND.

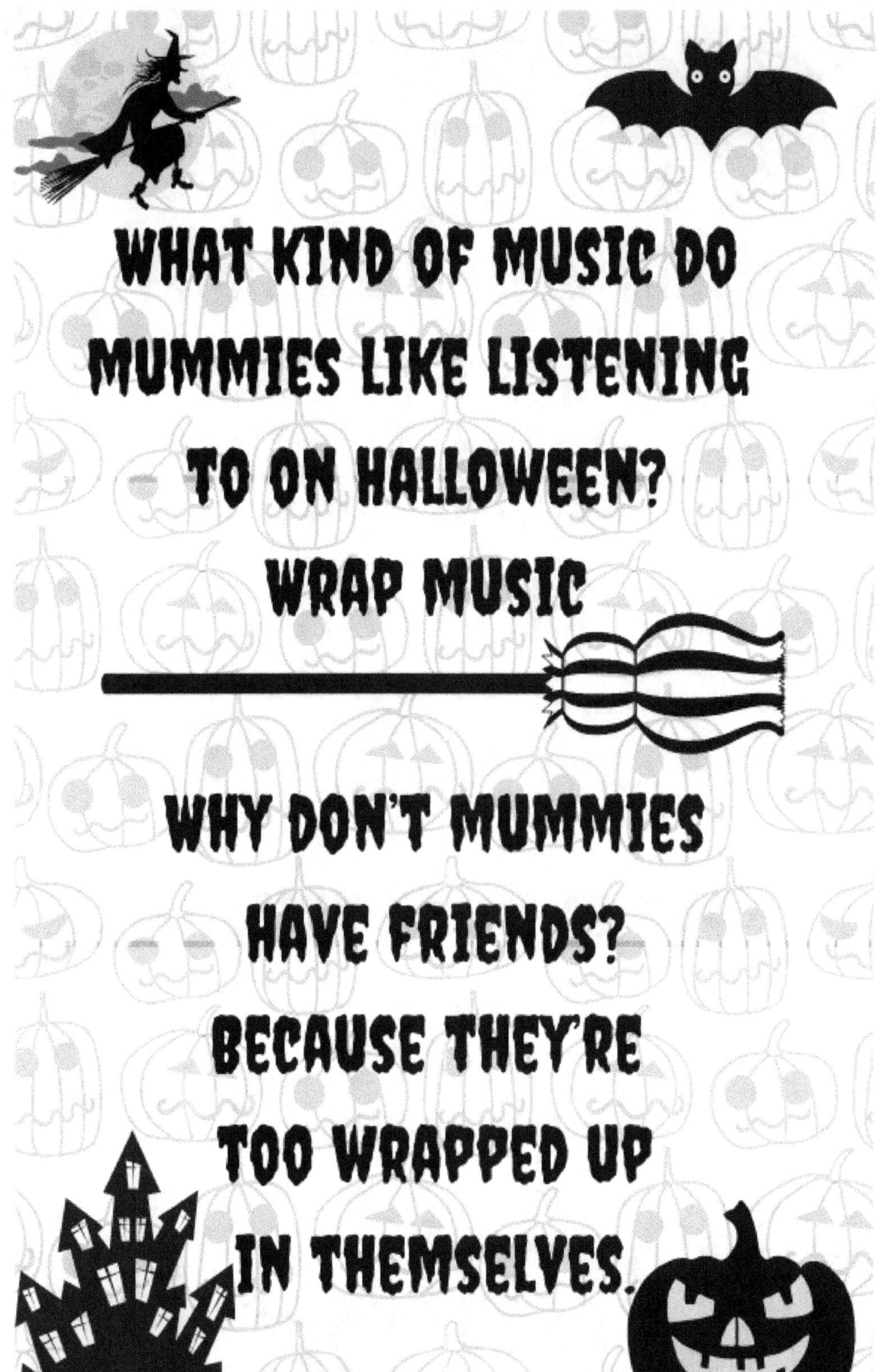

WHAT KIND OF MUSIC DO MUMMIES LIKE LISTENING TO ON HALLOWEEN?
WRAP MUSIC
WHY DON'T MUMMIES HAVE FRIENDS? BECAUSE THEY'RE TOO WRAPPED UP IN THEMSELVES.

WHAT HALLOWEEN CANDY IS NEVER ON TIME FOR THE PARTY?

CHOCO-LATE!

WHAT DO WITCHES PUT ON TO GO TRICK OR TREATING?

MAS-SCARE-A.

HAPPY
HALLOWEEN

trick or treat

HAPPY HALLOWEEN

HAPPY HALLOWEEN

HAPPY
HALLOWEEN

R.I.P.

HAPPY
HALLOWEEN